JIM CROCE

THE GREATEST HITS

CONTENTS

Transcribed and Arranged by YOICHI ARAKAWA

BAD, BAD LEROY BROWN

Words and Music by
JIM CROCE

Moderate boogie-rock

Intro:

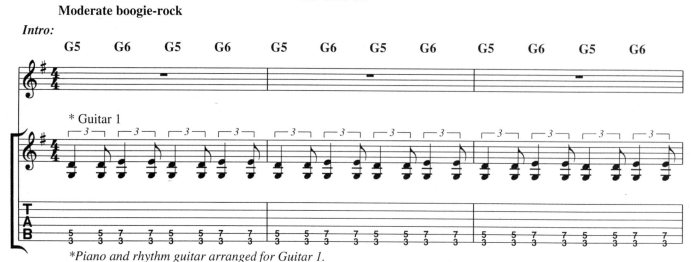

Piano and rhythm guitar arranged for Guitar 1.

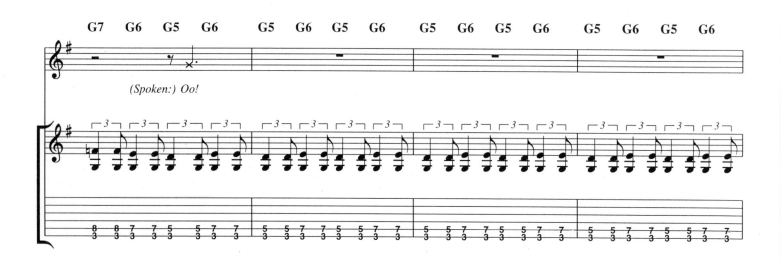

(Spoken:) Oo!

Verse 1:

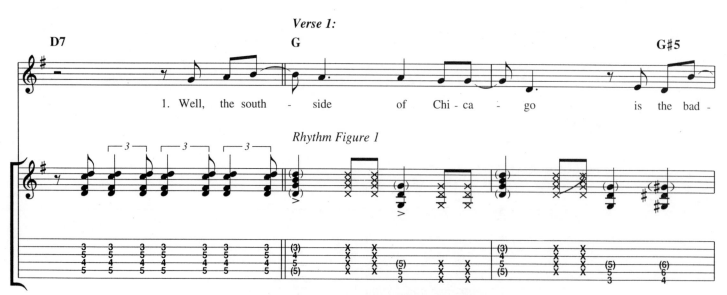

1. Well, the south - side of Chi - ca - go is the bad -

Rhythm Figure 1

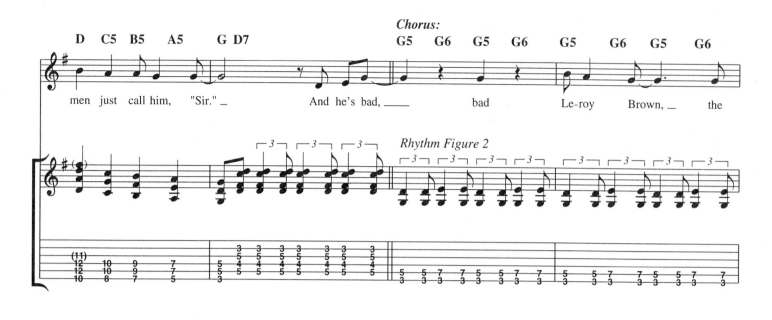

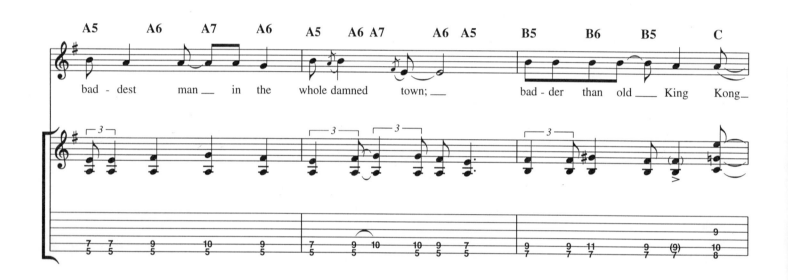

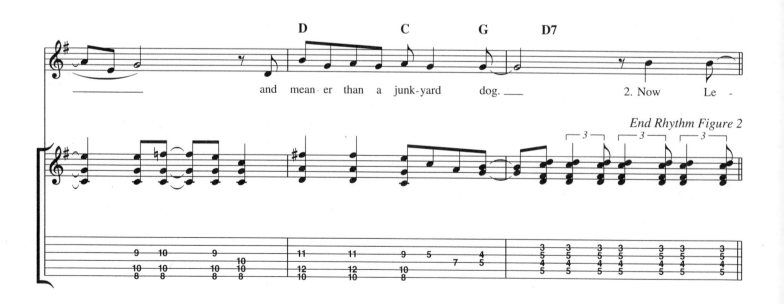

Verses 2 & 3: With Rhythm Figs. 1 & 2 w/ ad-lib variations

(3)*See additional lyrics*

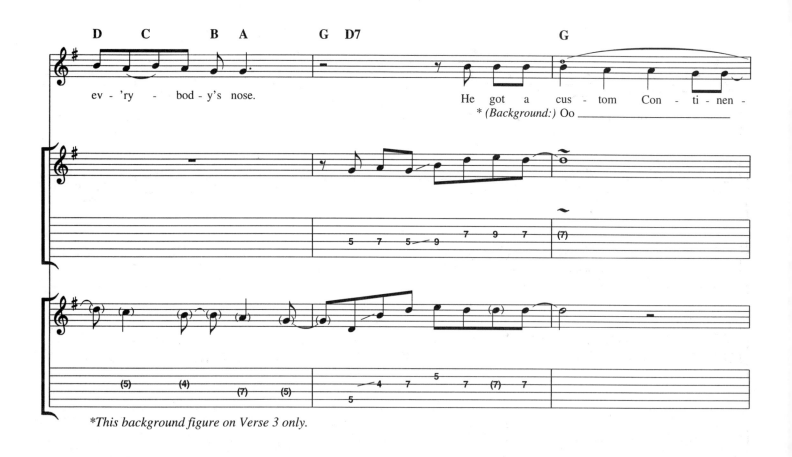

This background figure on Verse 3 only.

Chorus: With Rhythm Fig. 2 w/ ad-lib variations

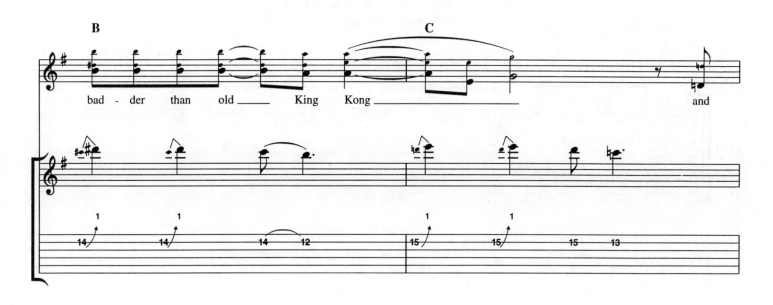

bad - der than old ___ King Kong _____ and

mean - er than a junk-yard dog. ___ Yeah, you were bad - der than old ___ King Kong, ___

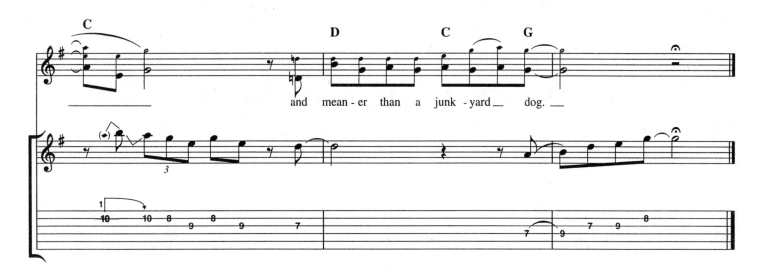

_____ and mean - er than a junk - yard ___ dog. ___

Additional lyrics

3. Well, Friday 'bout a week ago Leroy shootin' dice
And at the edge of the bar sat a girl name of Doris
And oh, that girl looked nice.
Well, he cast his eyes upon her, and the trouble soon began.
And Leroy Brown, he learned a lesson 'bout
Messin' with the wife of a jealous man.

(To Chorus:)

THESE DREAMS

Words and Music by
JIM CROCE

Verses 1 & 2:

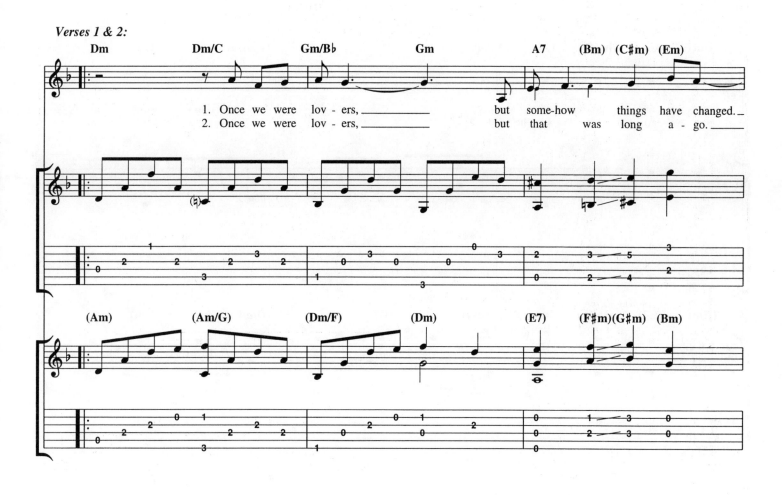

1. Once we were lov - ers, _____ but some-how things have changed. __
2. Once we were lov - ers, _____ but that was long a - go. _____

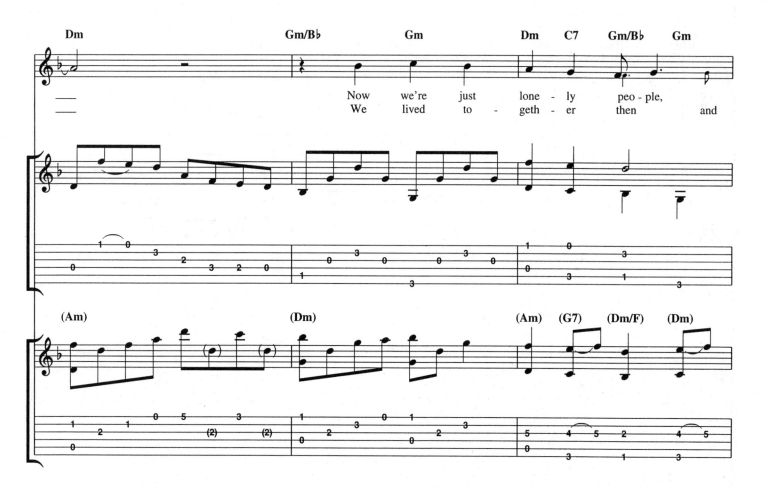

Now we're just lone - ly peo - ple,
We lived to - geth - er then and

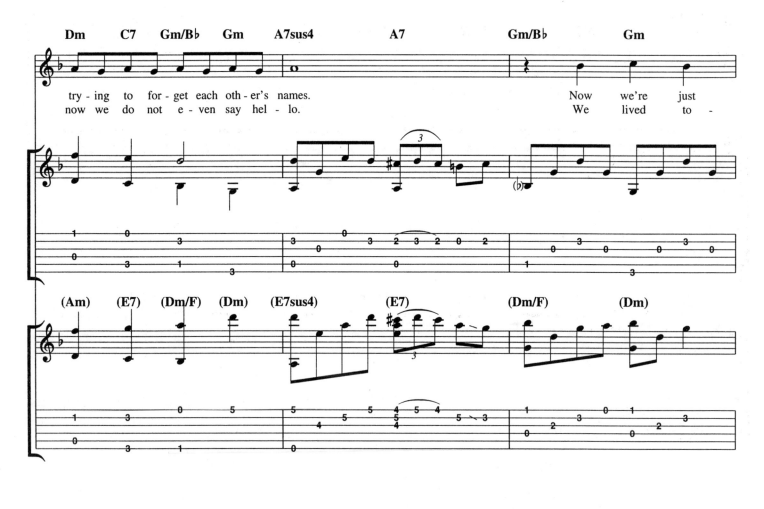

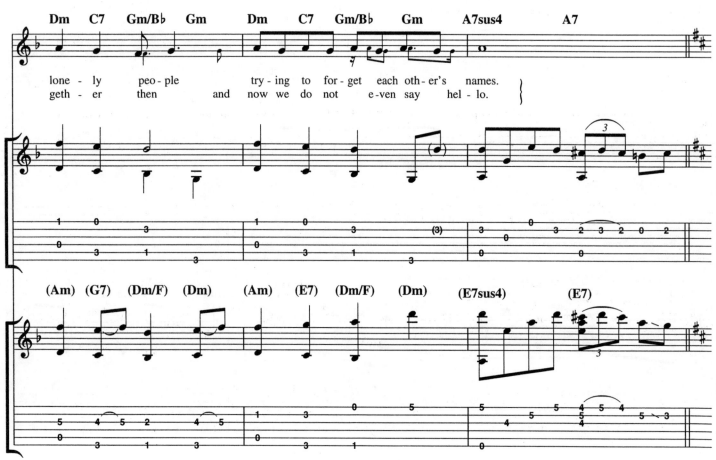

Chorus:

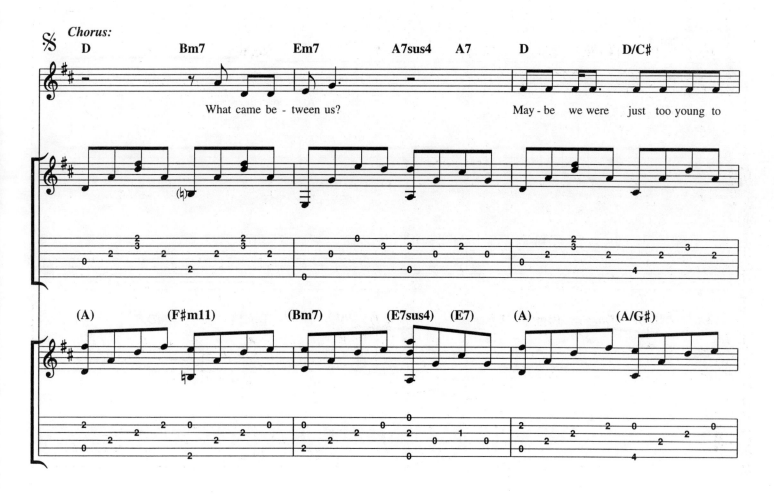

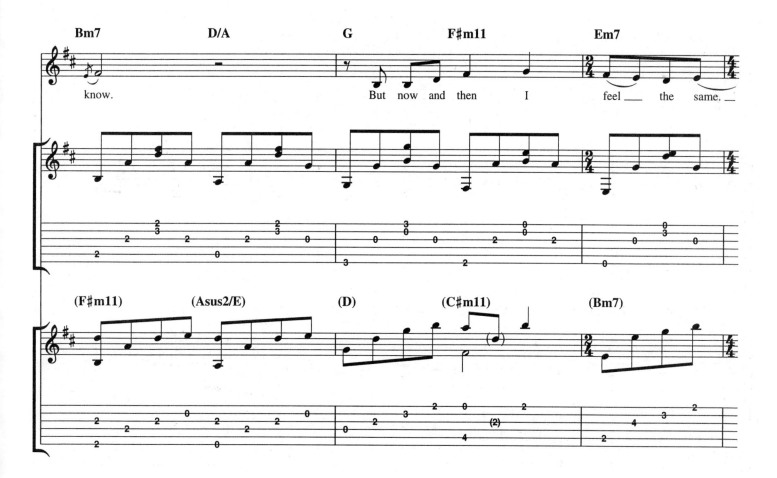

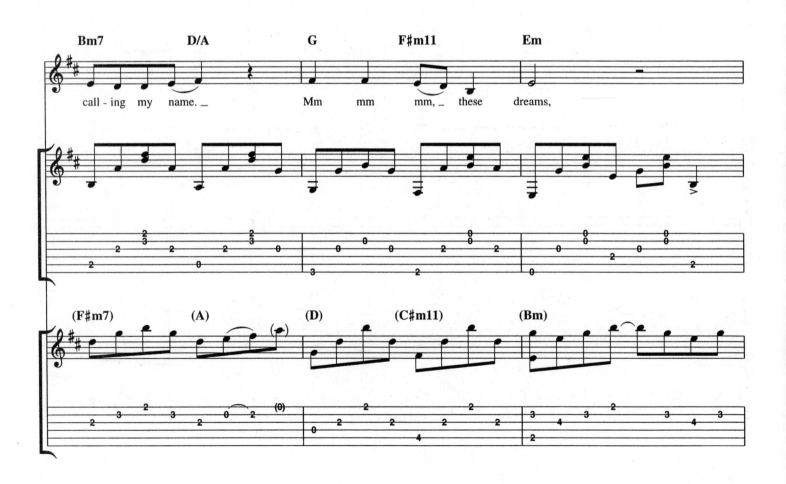

they keep me go - in' these days. __

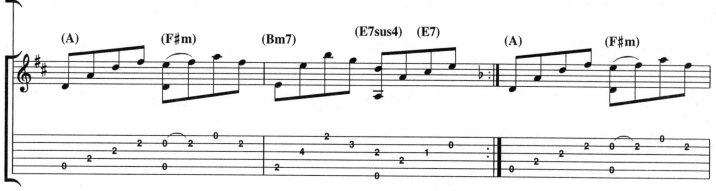

Interlude:
(With Strings)

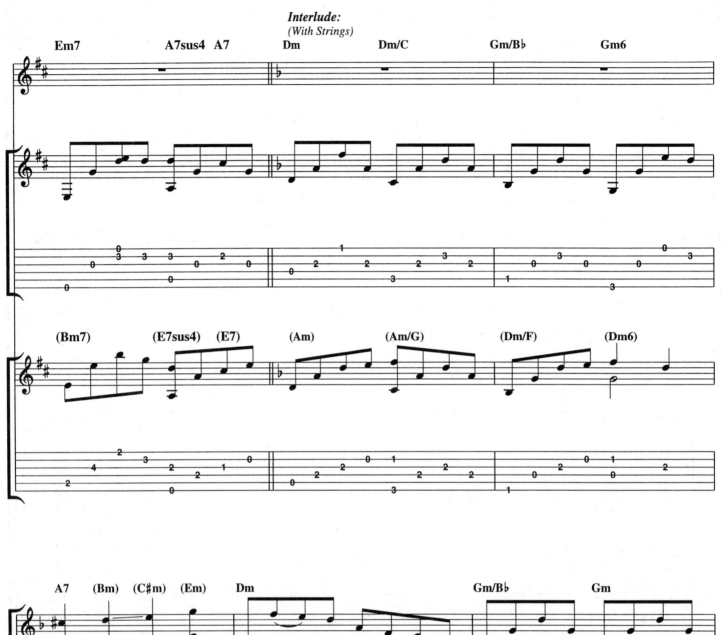

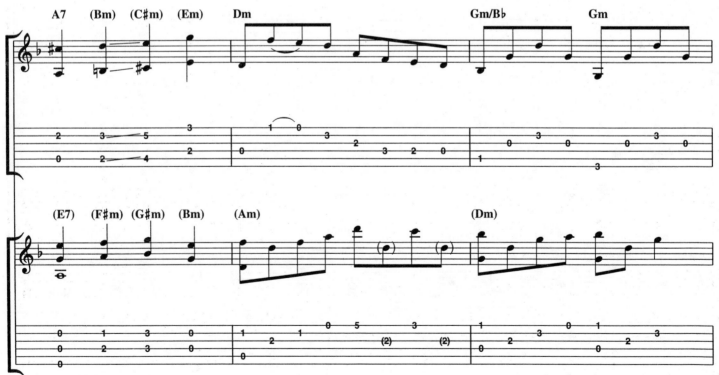

D.S. 𝄉 al Coda ⊕

TIME IN A BOTTLE

Words and Music by
JIM CROCE

Moderately
Intro:

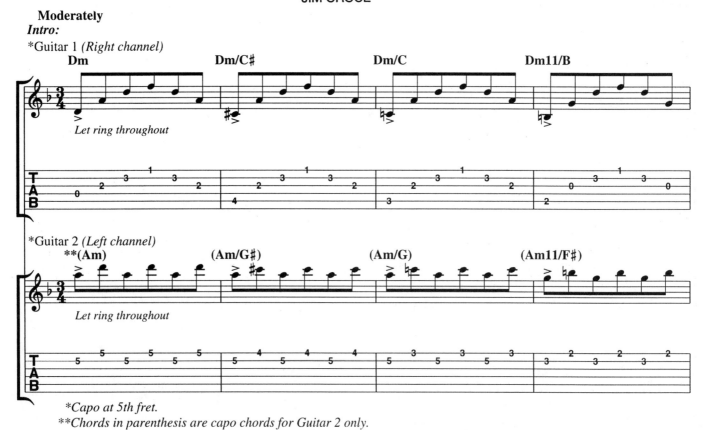

*Capo at 5th fret.
**Chords in parenthesis are capo chords for Guitar 2 only.

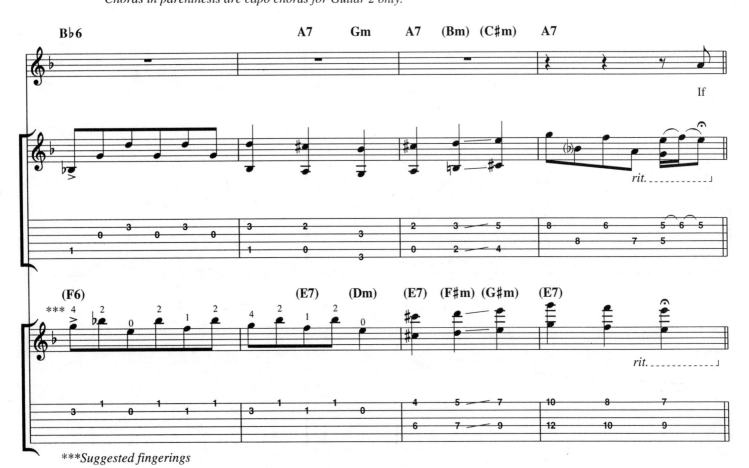

***Suggested fingerings

Verses:

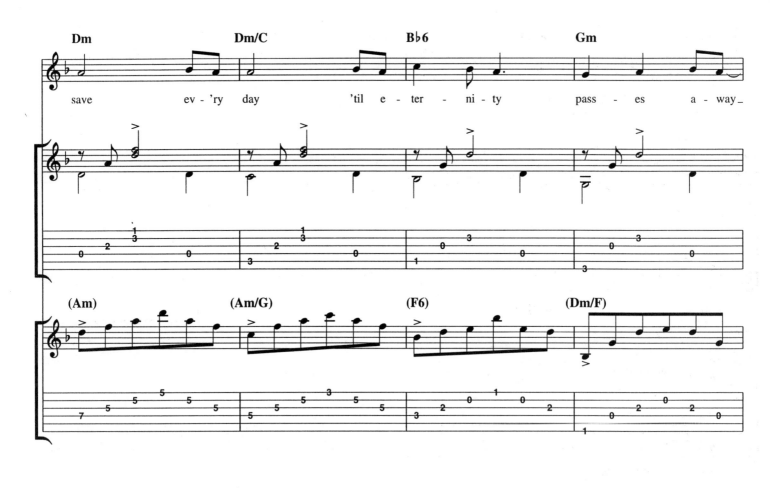

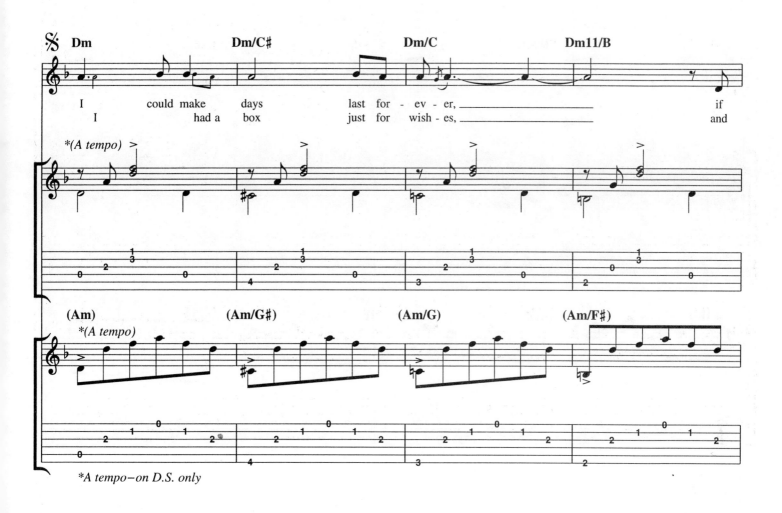

*A tempo–on D.S. only

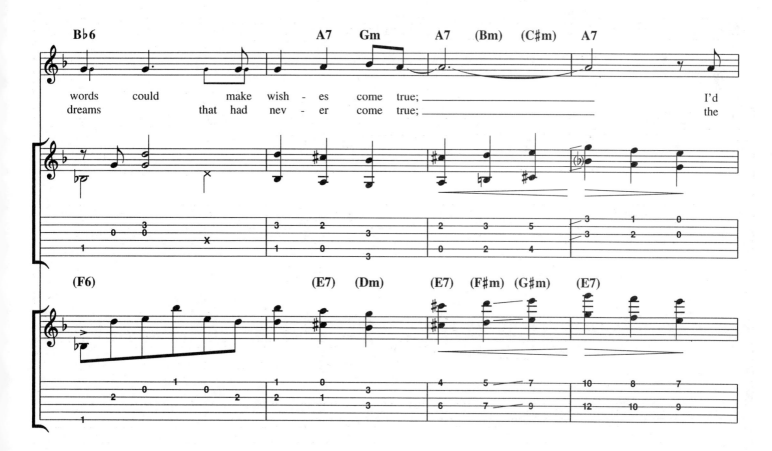

Chorus:

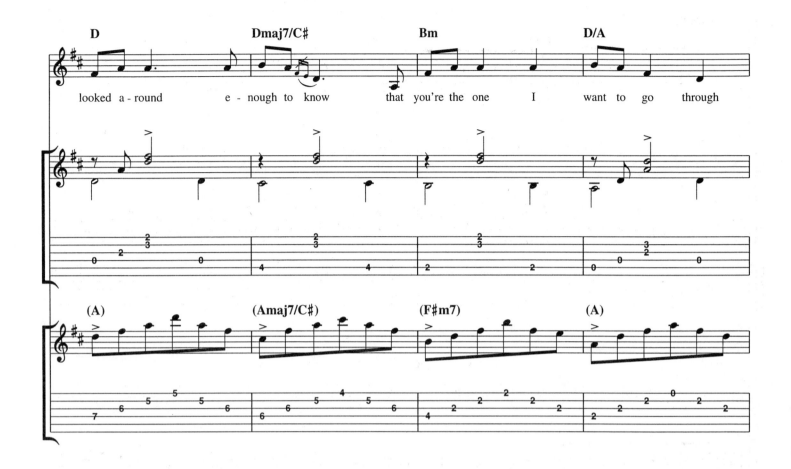

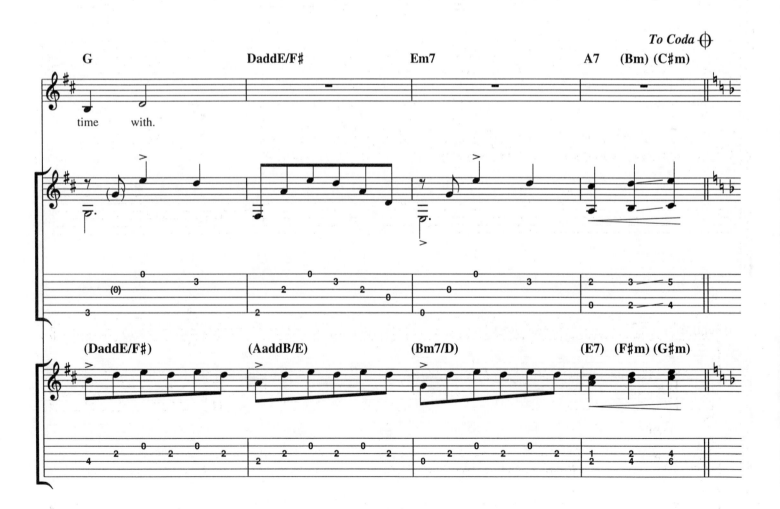

DREAMIN' AGAIN

Words and Music by
JIM CROCE

*Capo at 5th fret.
**Chords in parenthesis are capo chords for Guitar 2 only.
***Use fretted - string harmonics technique.

Verse 1:

know I ___ had a dream ___ last night ___ that you were here with me, ___

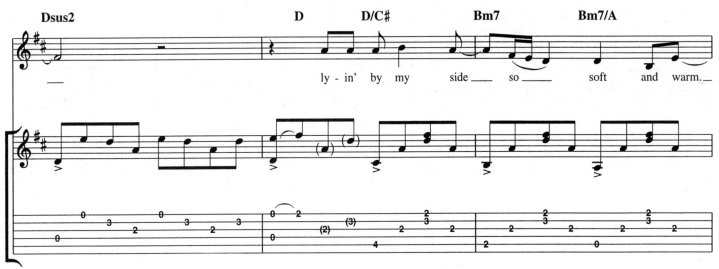

___ ly - in' by my side ___ so ___ soft and warm. ___

___ And we talked a - while ___ and

30

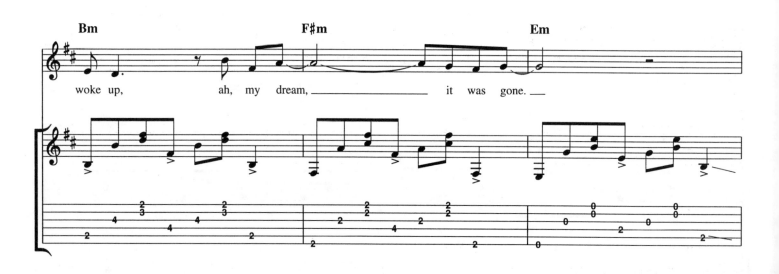

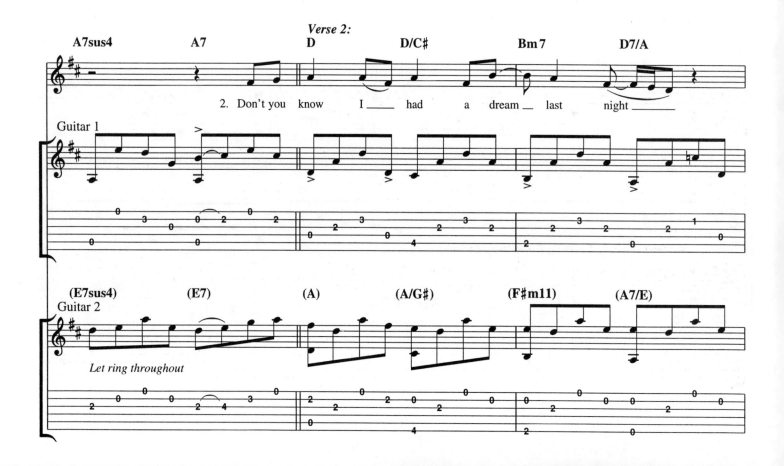

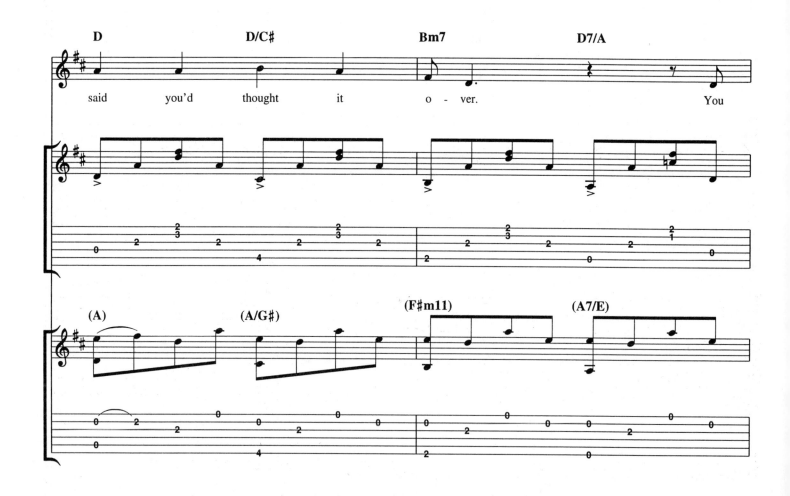

said   you'd   thought   it   o - ver.   You

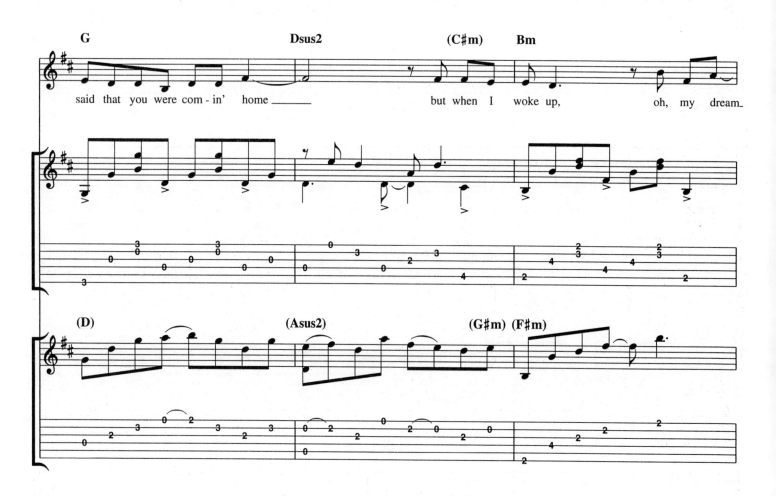

said that you were com-in' home _____ but when I woke up, oh, my dream_

it was gone.

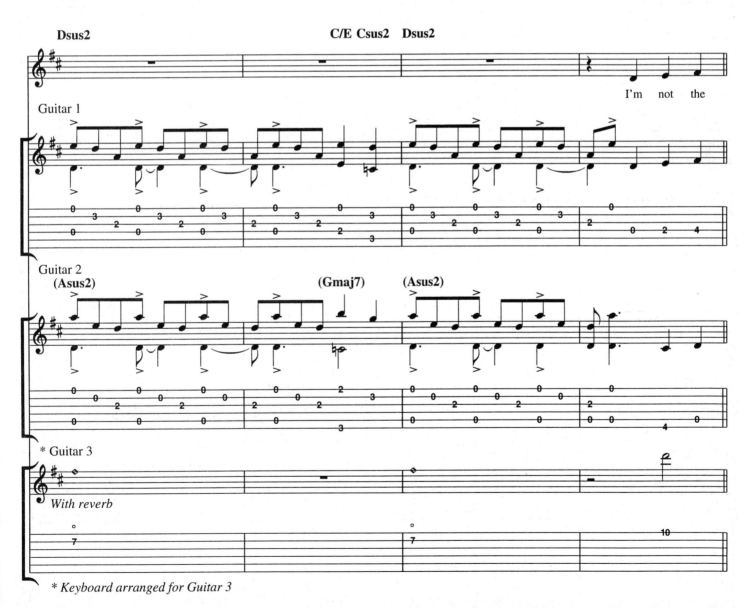

I'm not the

Guitar 1

Guitar 2

* Guitar 3

With reverb

*Keyboard arranged for Guitar 3

Chorus:

same. Can you blame me? Is it hard to un - der - stand?_ I can't for -

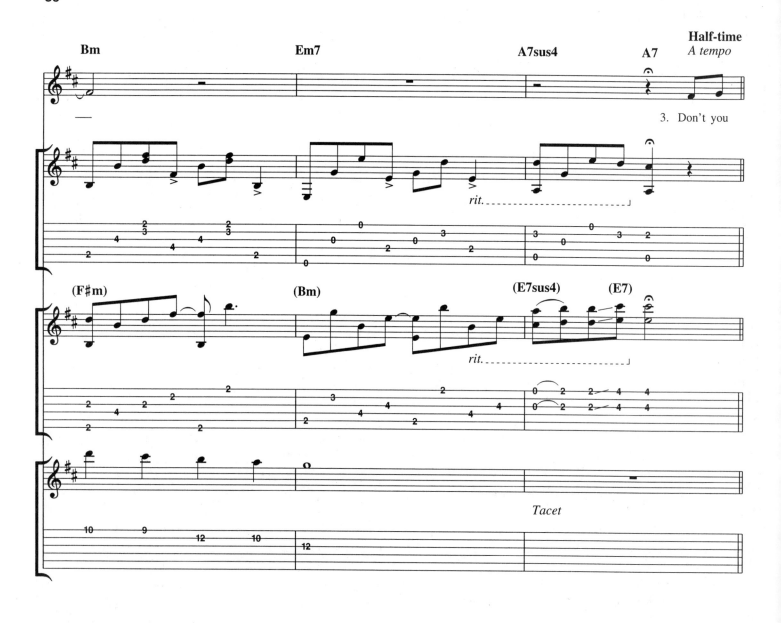

38

Outro:
Double-time

dream - in', _____ dream - in' a - gain.

I had been

I GOT A NAME

Words by
NORMAN GIMBEL

Music by
CHARLES FOX

Moderately

Intro:

Capo at 2nd fret.
**Chords in parenthesis are capo chords for Guitar 1 only.*

Verses 1, 2, & 3:

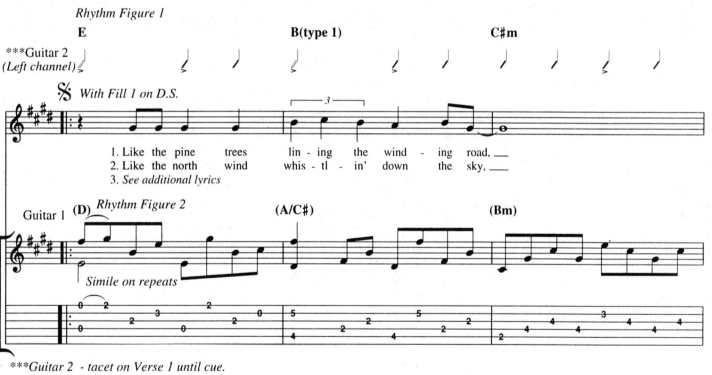

1. Like the pine trees lin - ing the wind - ing road, ___
2. Like the north wind whis - tl - in' down the sky, ___
3. *See additional lyrics*

***Guitar 2 - tacet on Verse 1 until cue.*

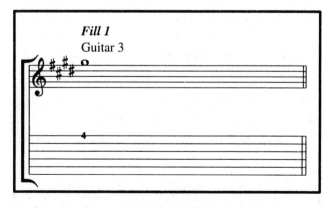

*Doubled by a 12-string acoustic guitar.

I've got a name. ___
I've got a song. ___

Guitar 2 *(on Verse 1 only)*

End Rhythm Figure 1 **G♯m**

And I car - ry it with ___ me like my
And I car - ry it with ___ me and I

End Rhythm Figure 2

dad - dy   did, ___   but I'm liv - ing the   dream ___
sing it   loud; ___   if   it   gets   me   no - where, _____

that   he   kept   hid. _____
I'll   go   there   proud. _____

(Gtr. 2 continues to slash notation)

Chorus:

Bass arranged for Guitar 1 for next six bars.

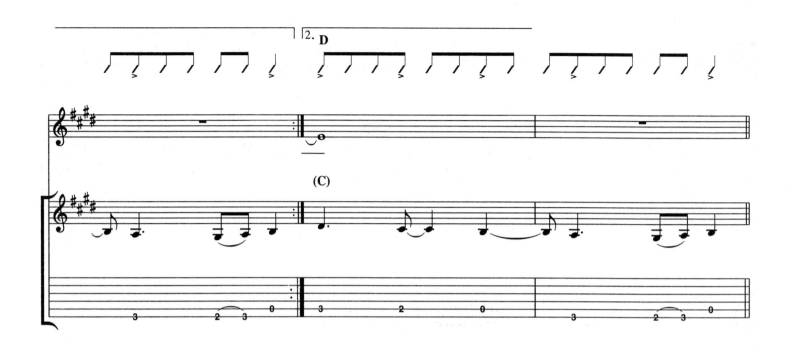

Guitar Solo: With Rhythm Figs. 1 & 2 w/ad-lib variations

Guitar 3

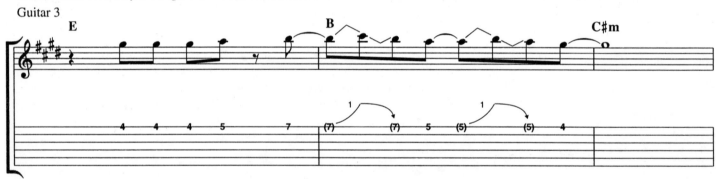

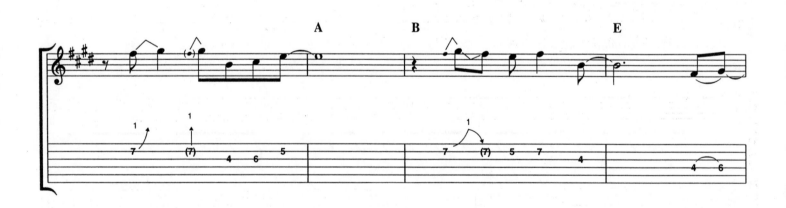

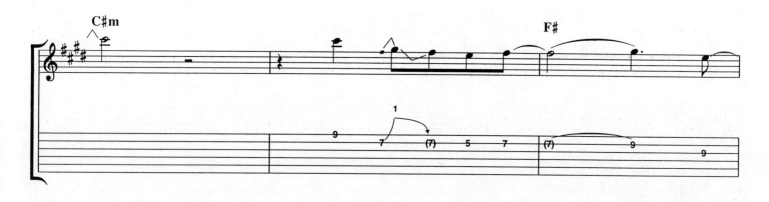

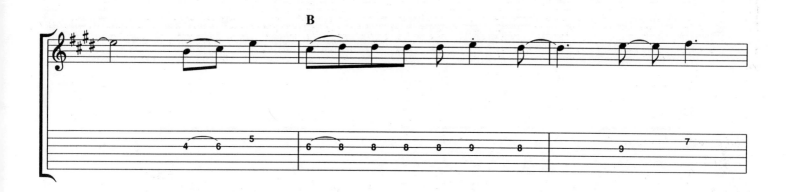

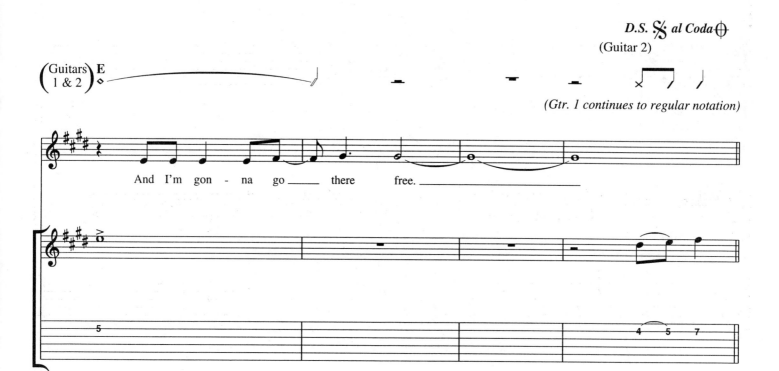

Additional lyrics

3. Like the fool I am and I'll always be,
   I've got a dream; I've got a dream.
   They can change their minds, but they can't change me,
   I've got a dream; I've got a dream.
   Oh, I know I could share it if you'd want me to;
   If you're goin' my way, I'll go with you.

   Movin' me down the highway,
   Rollin' me down the highway,
   Movin' ahead so life won't pass me by.

I'LL HAVE TO SAY I LOVE YOU IN A SONG

Words and Music by
JIM CROCE

Moderately
Intro:

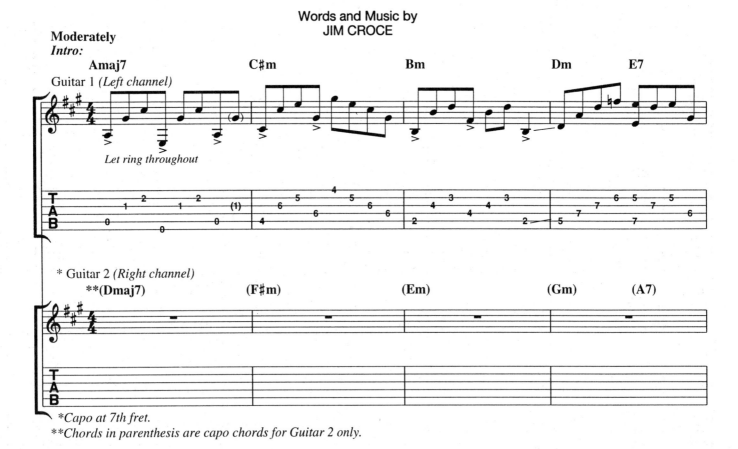

*Capo at 7th fret.
**Chords in parenthesis are capo chords for Guitar 2 only.

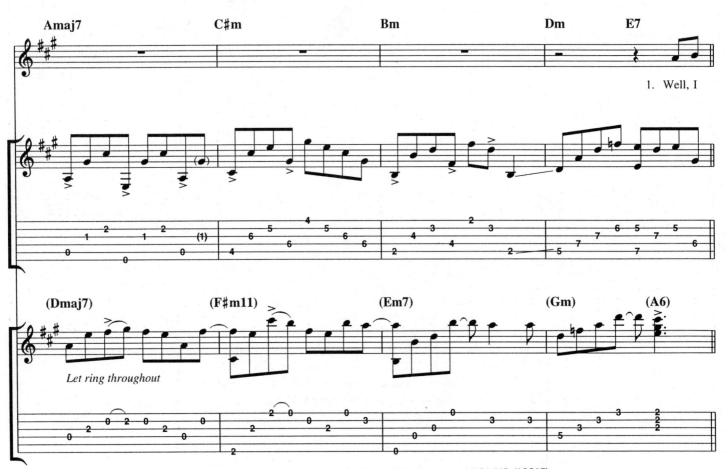

1. Well, I

Verses 1 & 2:
With Fill 1 on Verse 2

Amaj7   C#m   Bm

know it's kind of late ___ I hope I did-n't wake ___
(2.) know it's kind of strange ___ but ev-'ry time I'm near ___

(Dmaj7)   (F#m11)   (Em7)

E   (F#m)   (G#m)   Amaj7   C#m

___ you. But what I got to say ___ can't wait. ___
___ you, I just run out of things ___ to say. ___

(A)   (Dmaj7)   (F#m11)

Fill 1
Guitar 2

Chorus:

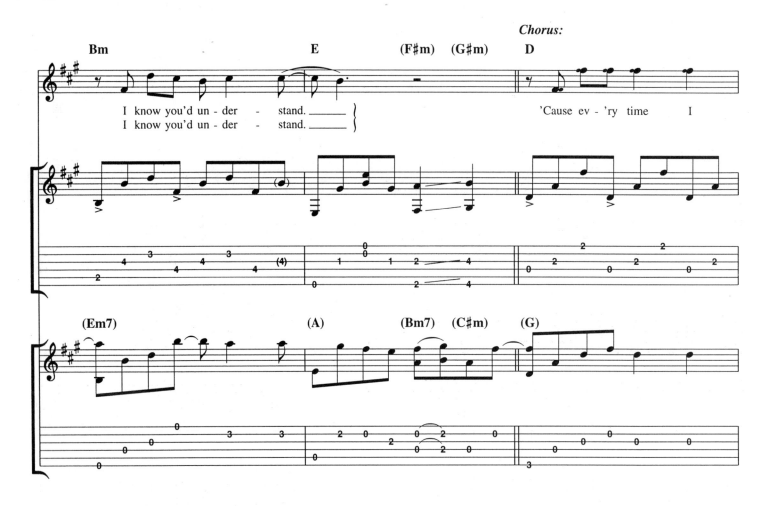

I know you'd un - der - stand. _____ 'Cause ev - 'ry time I
I know you'd un - der - stand. _____

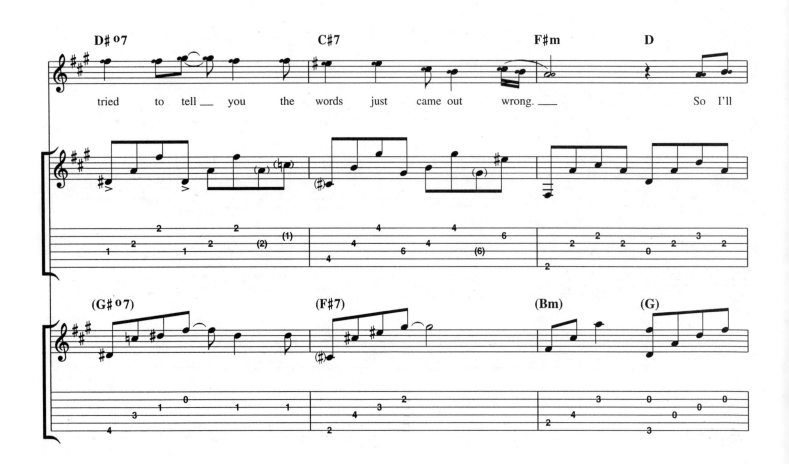

tried to tell __ you the words just came out wrong. ___ So I'll

have   to   say ___   I   love ___   you   in   a   song.

2. Yeah, I   song.

Guitar Solo:

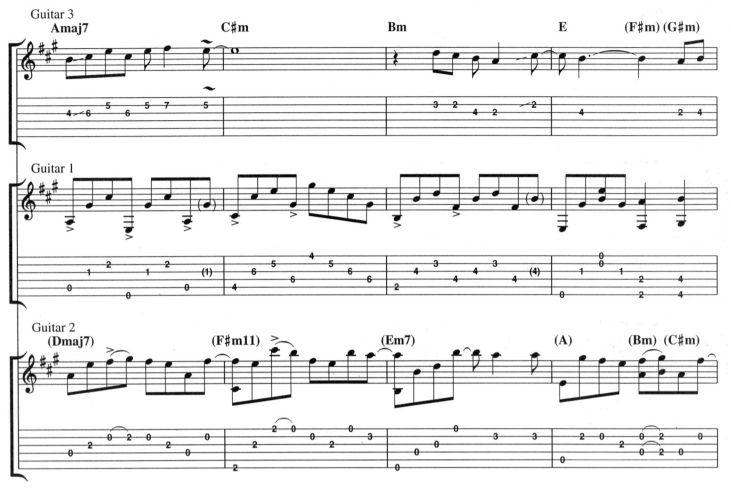

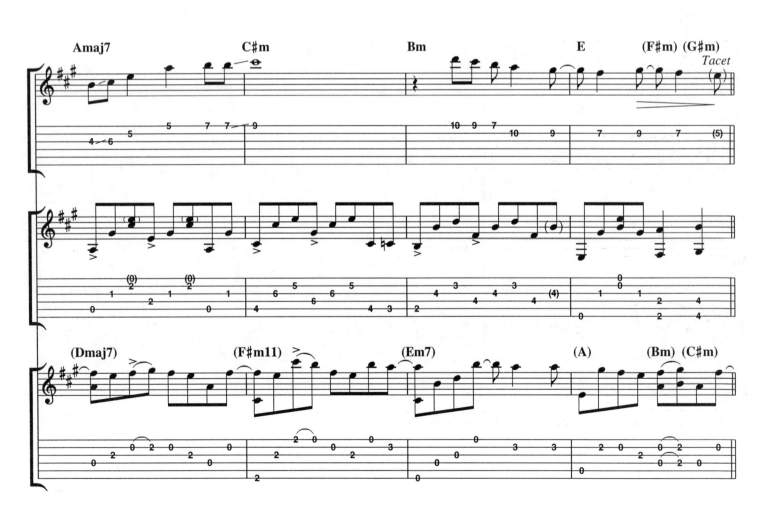

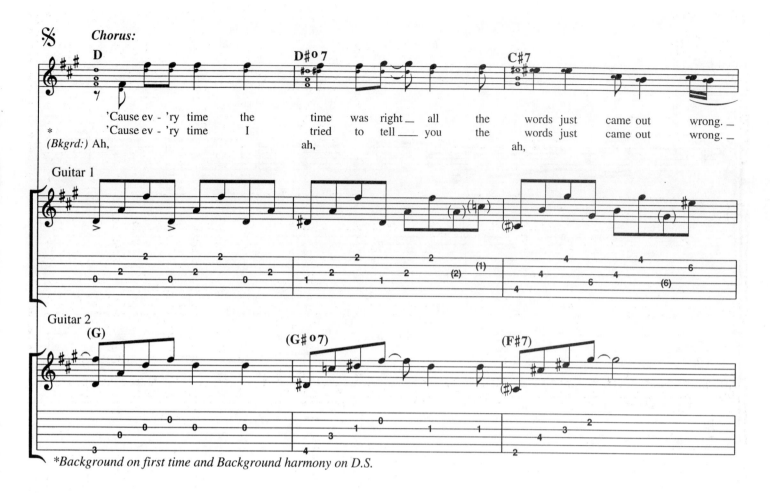

*Background on first time and Background harmony on D.S.

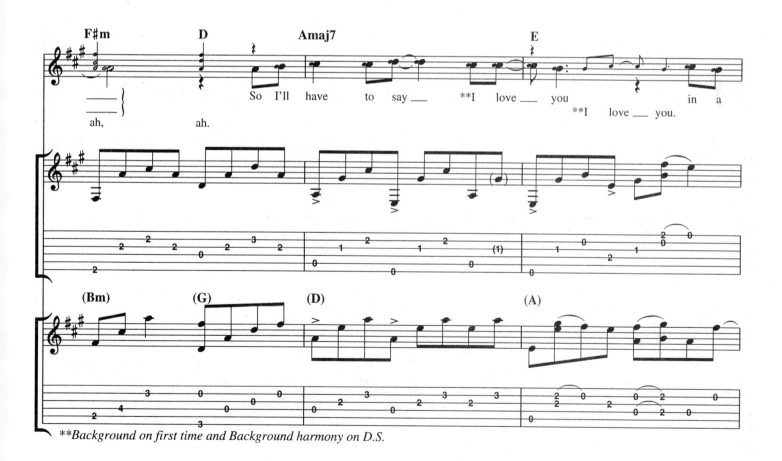

**Background on first time and Background harmony on D.S.

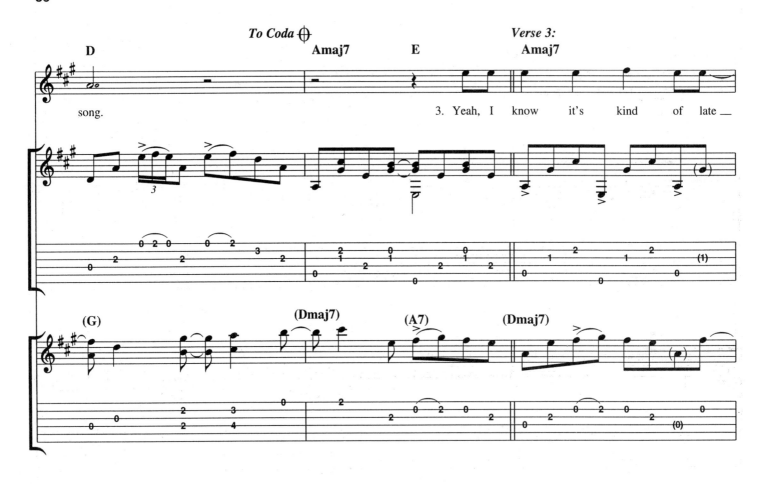

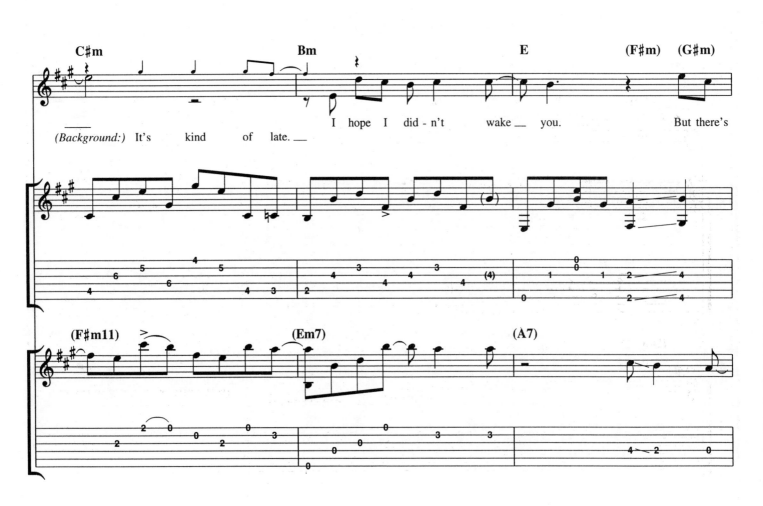

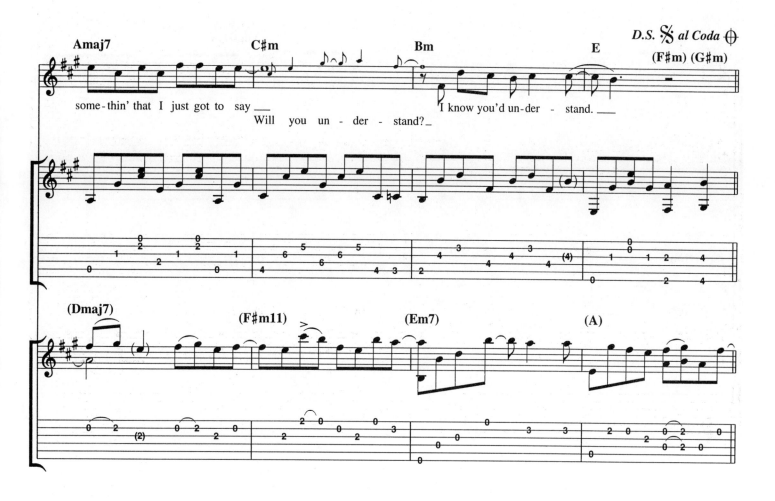

some-thin' that I just got to say ___ Will you un-der-stand? _ I know you'd un-der - stand. ___

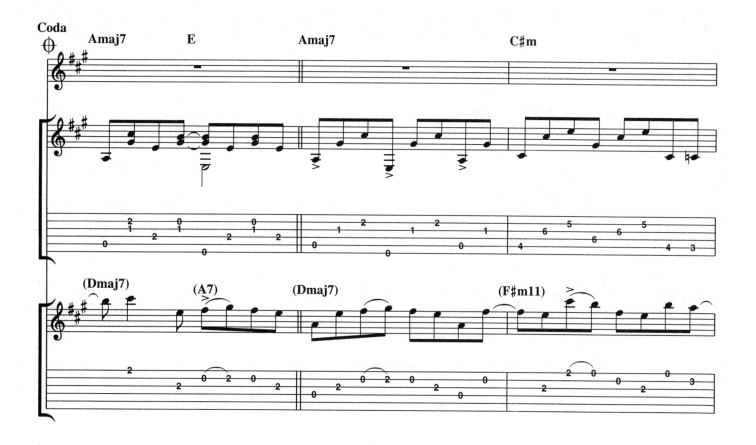

58

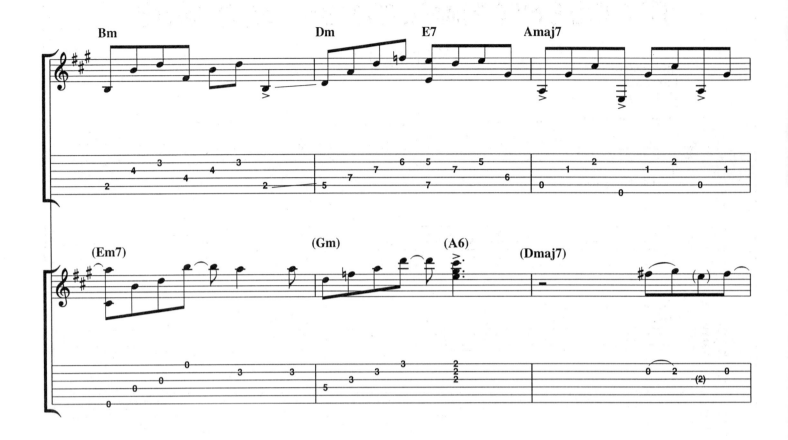

IT DOESN'T HAVE TO BE THAT WAY

Words and Music by
JIM CROCE

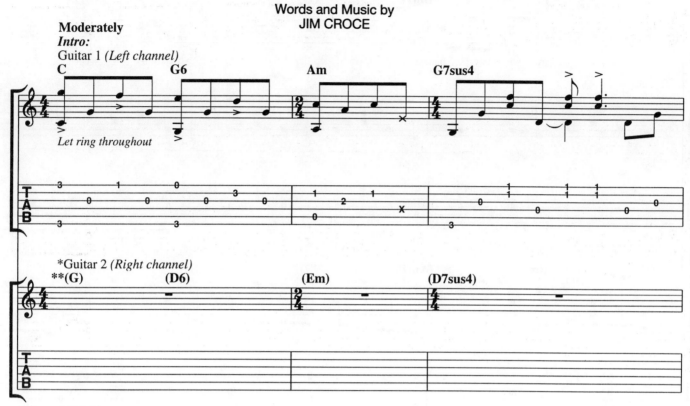

*Capo at 5th fret.

**Chords in parenthesis are capo chords for Guitar 2 only.

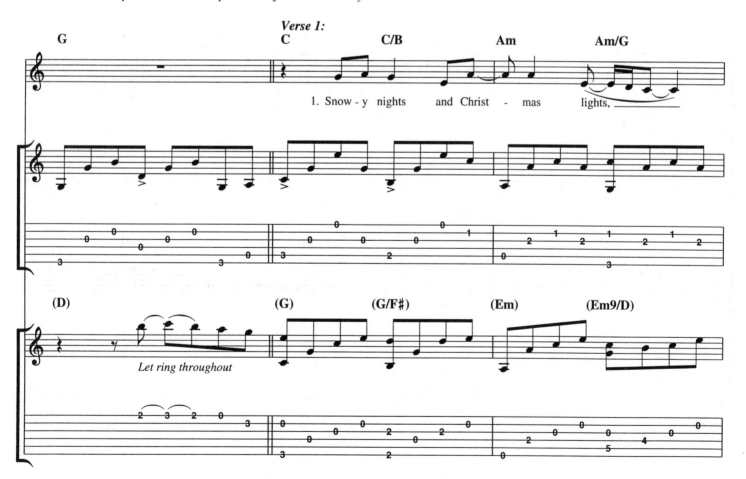

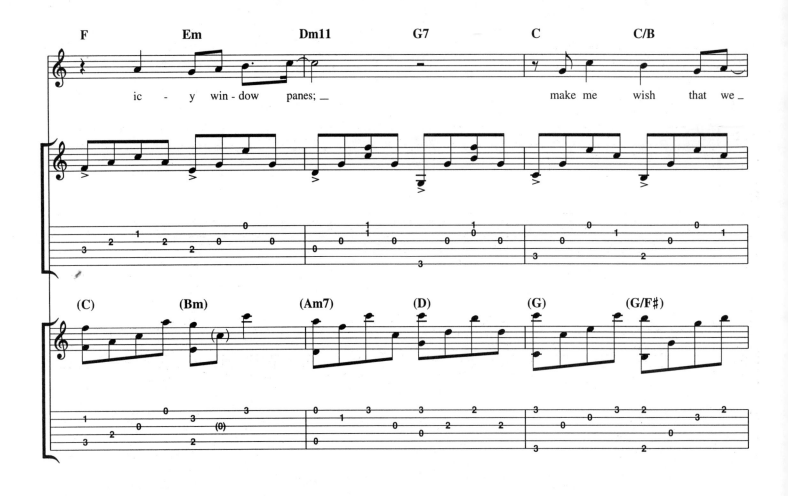

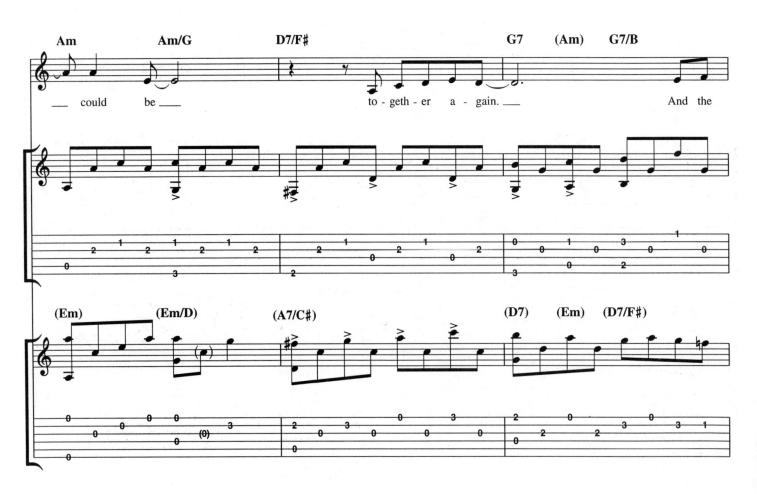

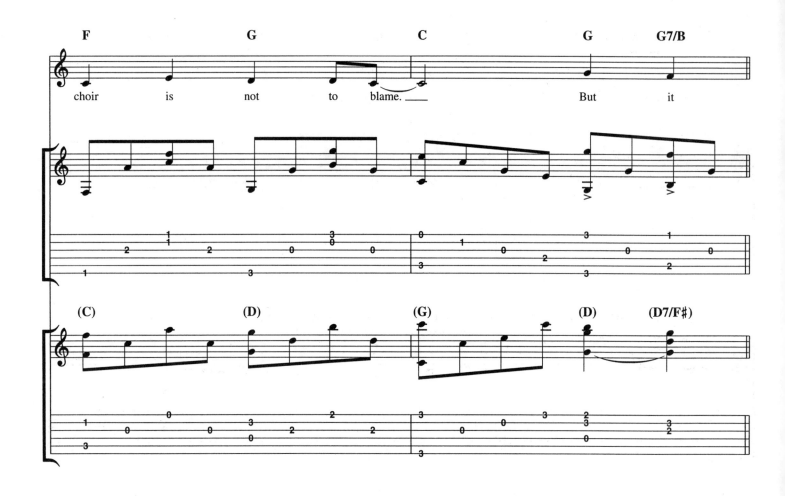

Chorus:

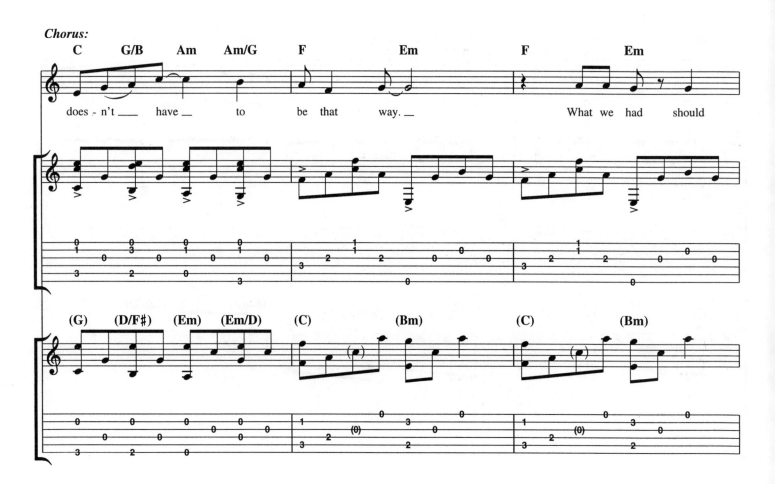

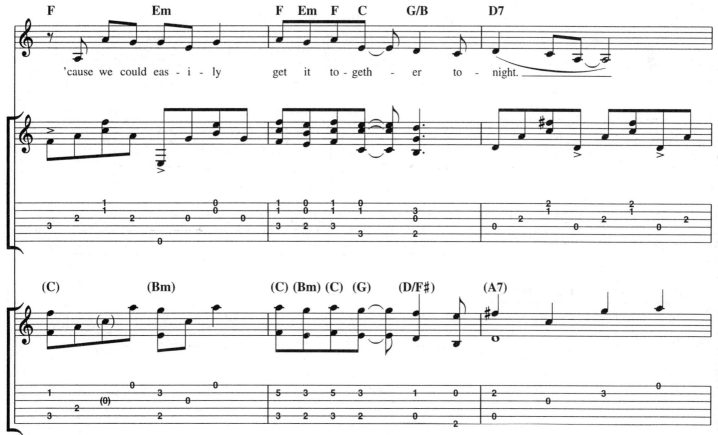

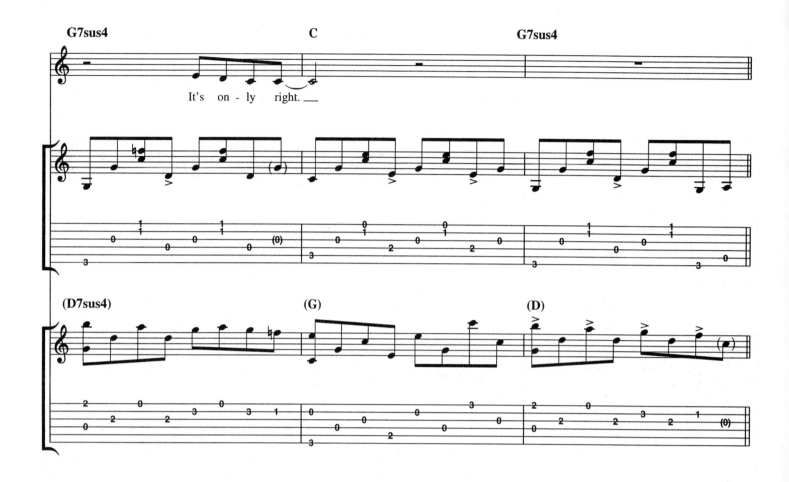

Verse 2:

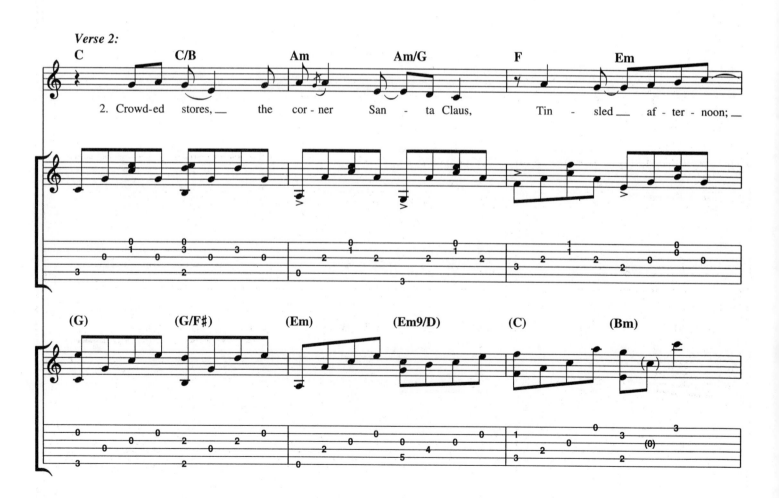

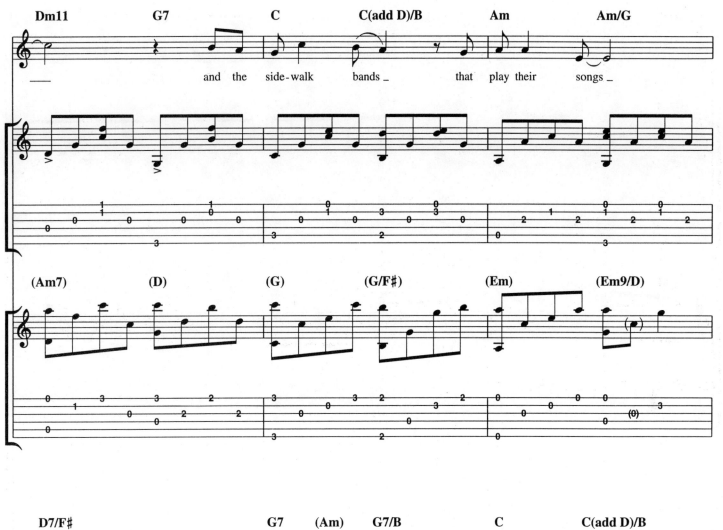

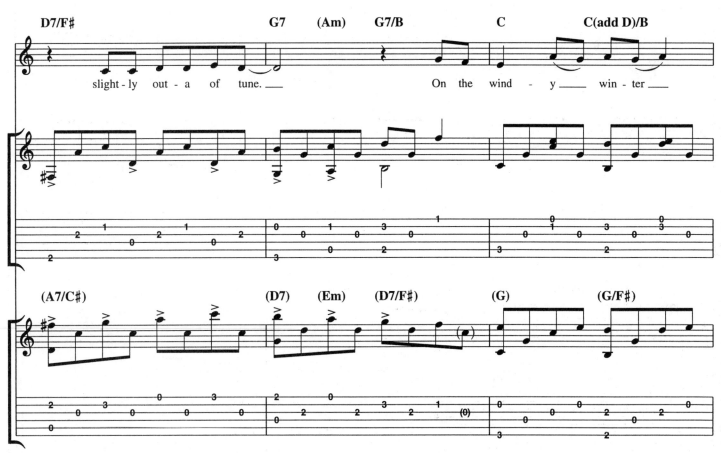

Chorus:

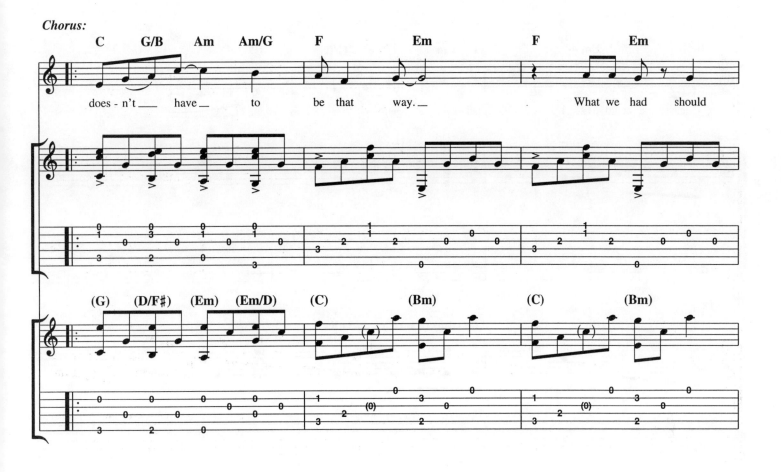

does - n't ___ have ___ to be that way. ___ What we had should

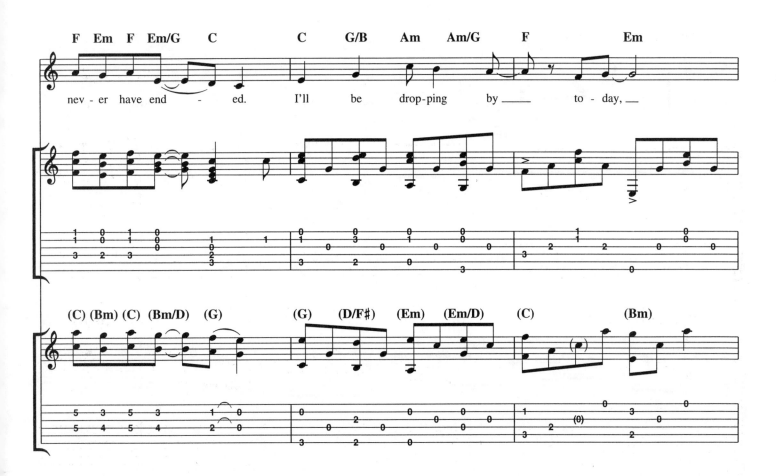

nev - er have end - ed. I'll be drop-ping by ___ to - day, ___

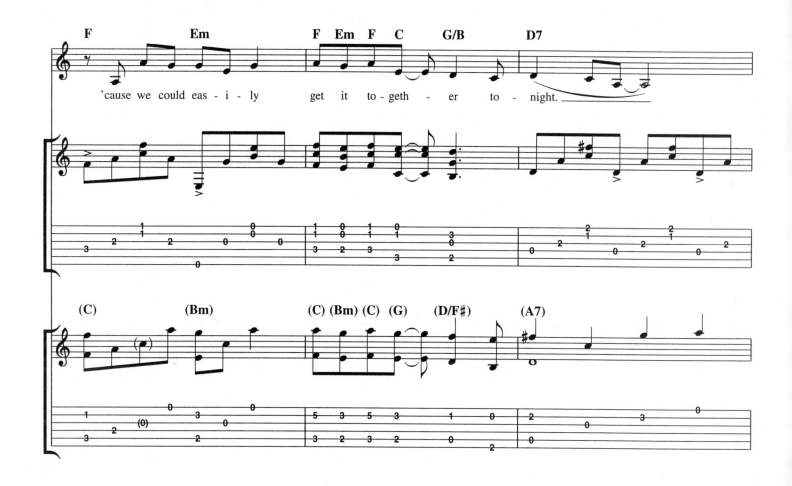

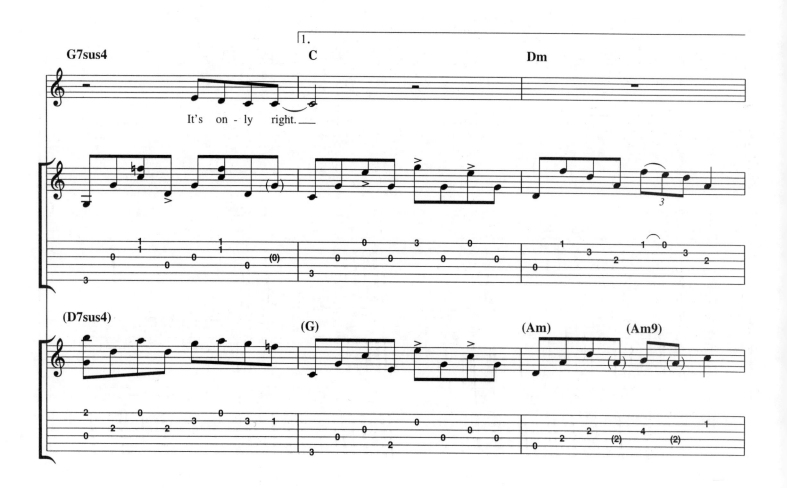

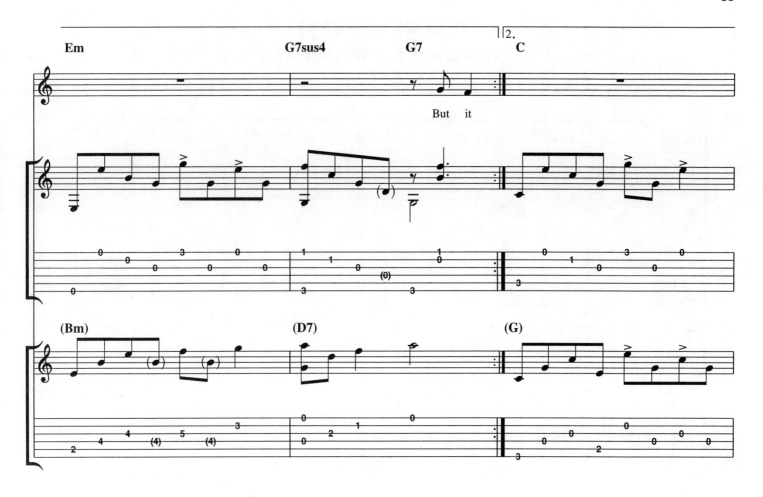

But it

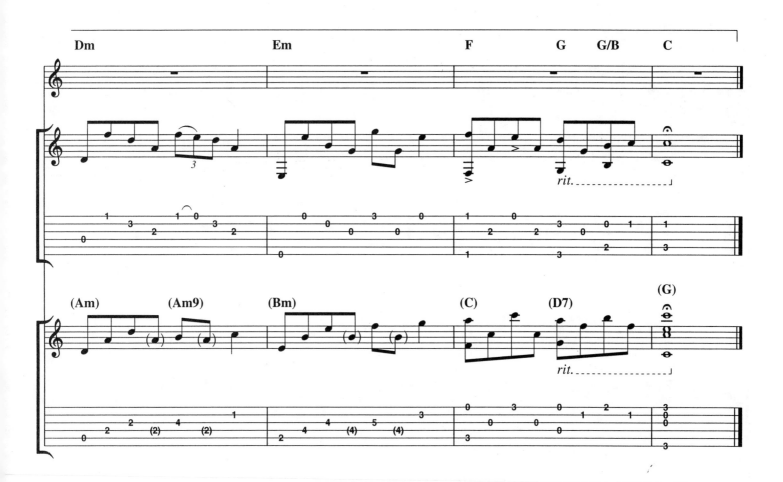

OPERATOR
(That's Not The Way It Feels)

Words and Music by
JIM CROCE

*Capo at 5th fret.
**Chords in parenthesis are capo chords for Guitar 2 only.

*Harmony backgrounds on Verses 2 & 3 only.

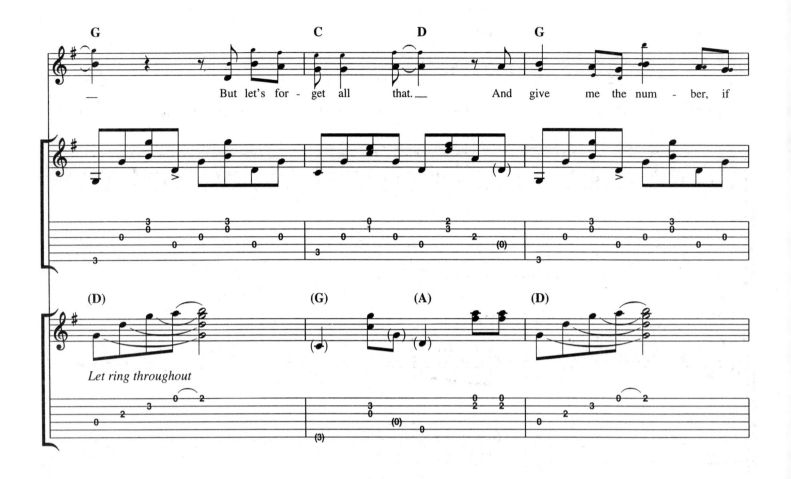

But that's not the way it feels.

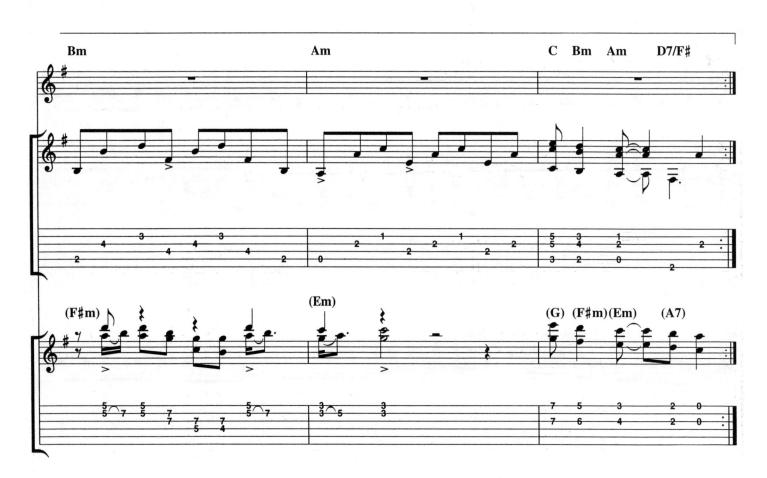

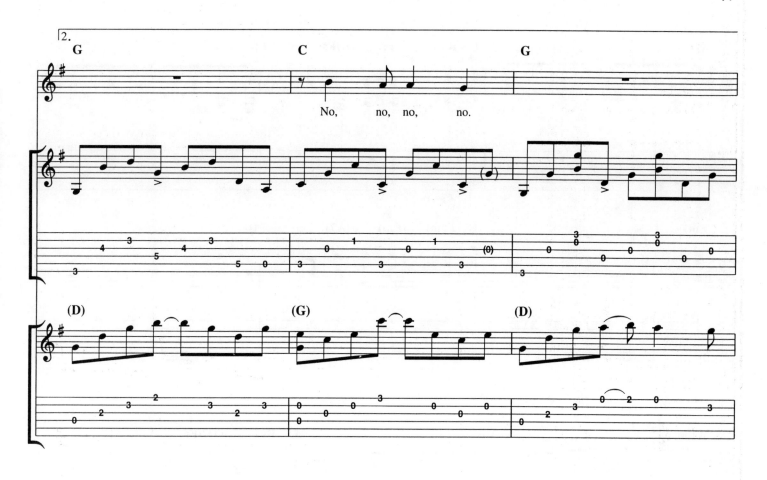

No, no, no, no.

That's not the way it

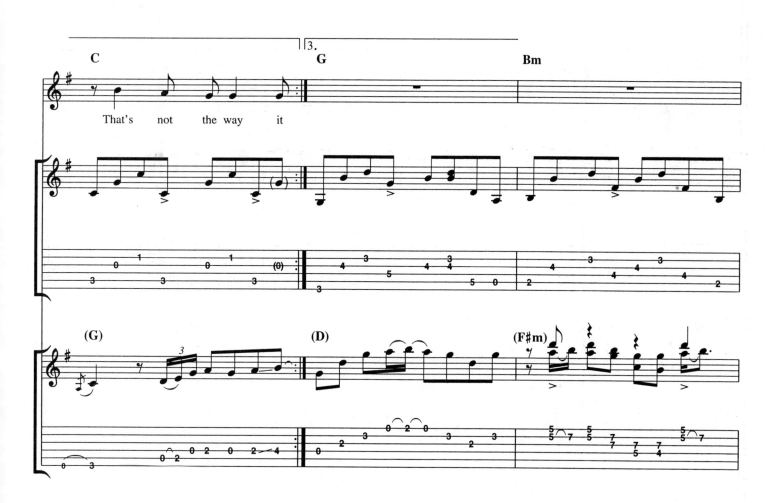

78

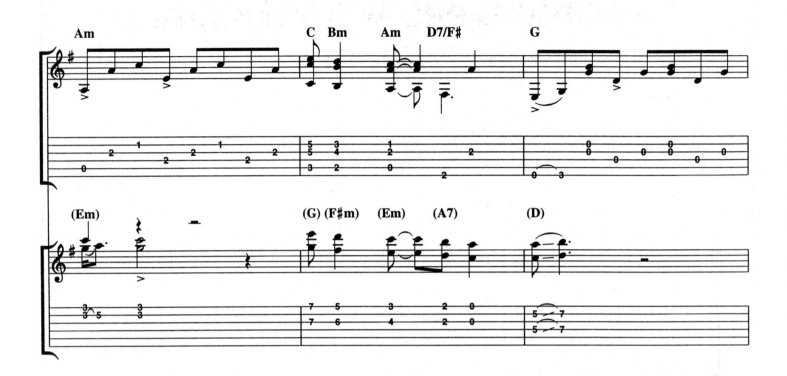

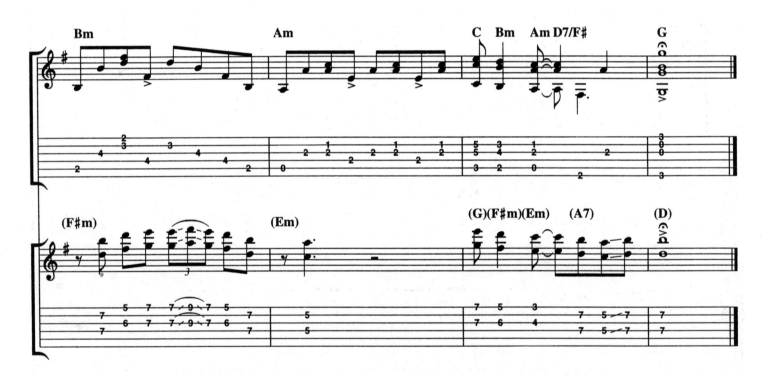

Additional lyrics

2. Operator, oh could you help me place this call?
'Cause I can't read the number that you just gave me.
There's something in my eyes,
You know it happens every time;
I think about the love that I thought would save me.

(To Chorus:)

3. Operator, oh let's forget about this call.
(There's) no one there I really wanted to talk to.
Thank you for your time.
Oh, you've been so much more than kind
You can keep your dime.

(To Chorus:)

PHOTOGRAPHS AND MEMORIES

Words and Music by
JIM CROCE

80

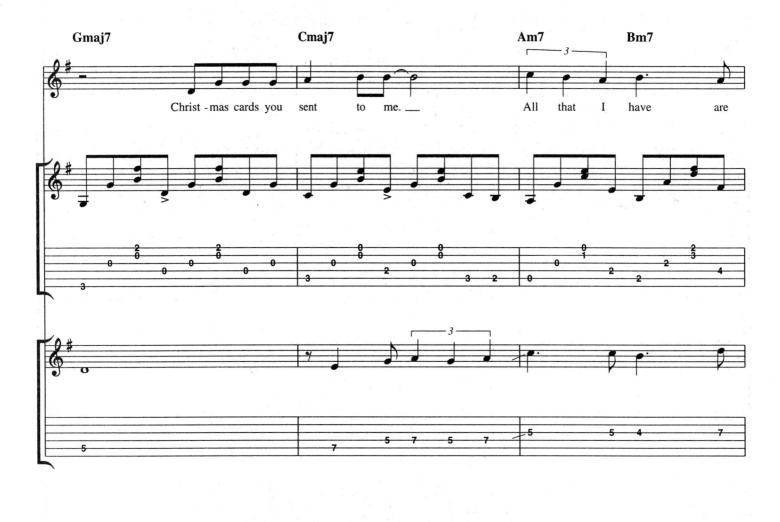

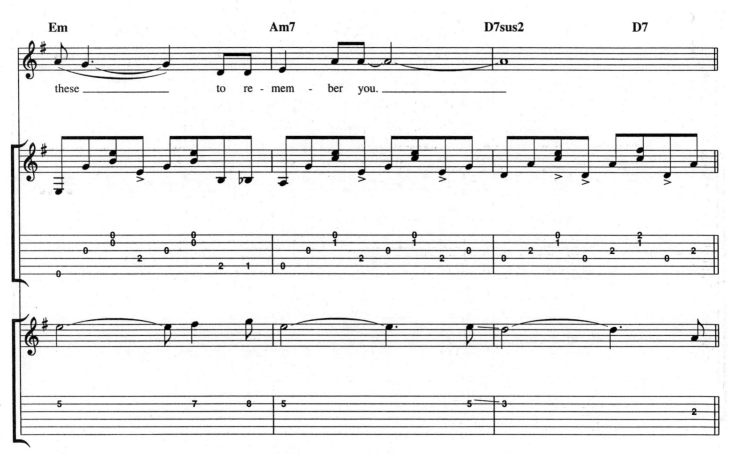

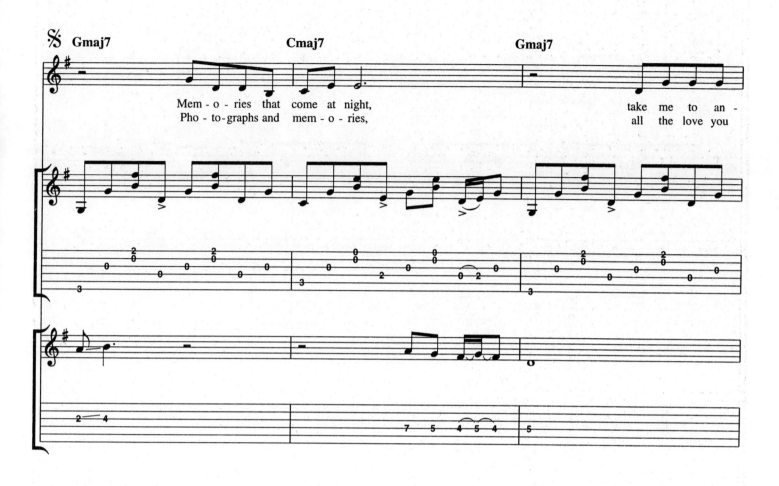

Verse:
*A tempo

*To the original tempo

Sum-mer skies and lul - la - bies, nights we could-n't

say good - bye; ___ and of all of the things that we knew _____ not a

Am7   D7sus2   D7   *Interlude:*
                                                        Gmaj7

dream   sur - vived. _____

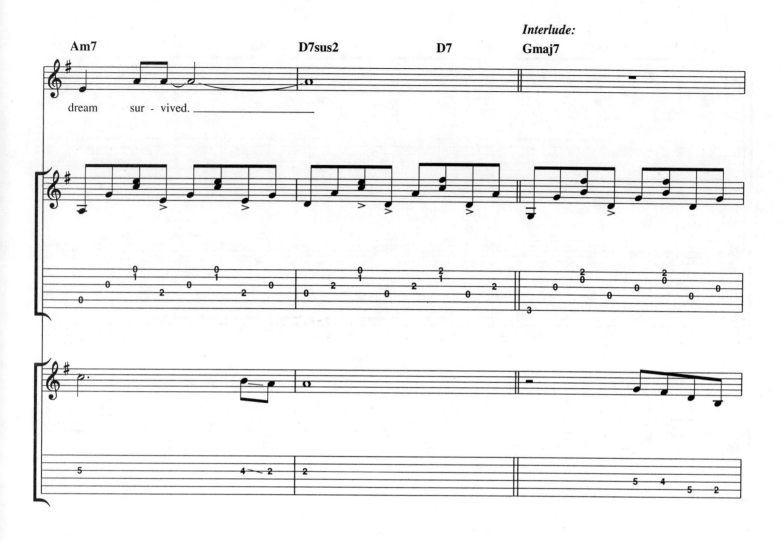

Cmaj7   Gmaj7   Cmaj7

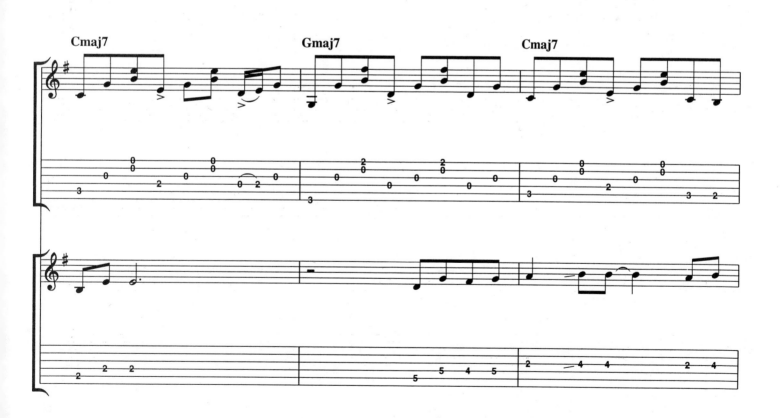

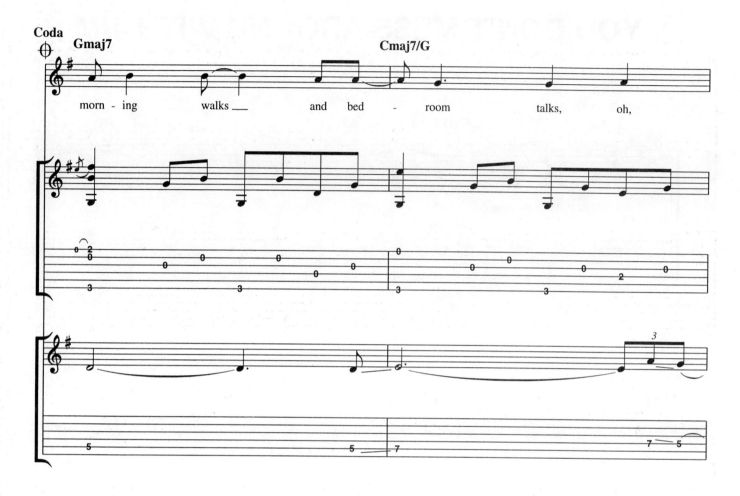

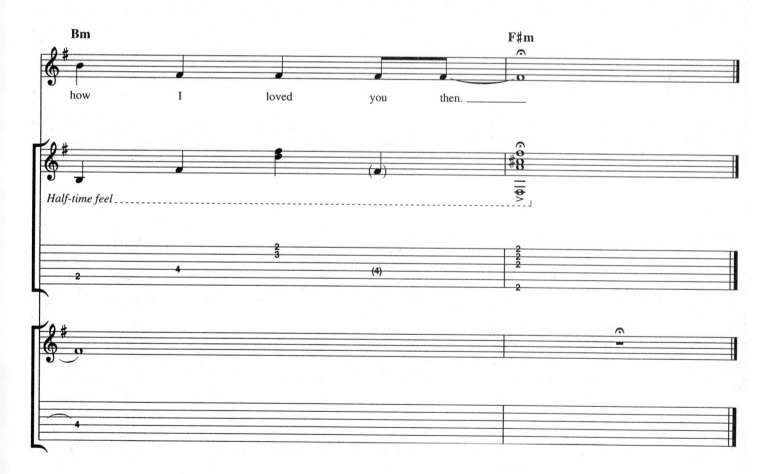

YOU DON'T MESS AROUND WITH JIM

Words and Music by
JIM CROCE

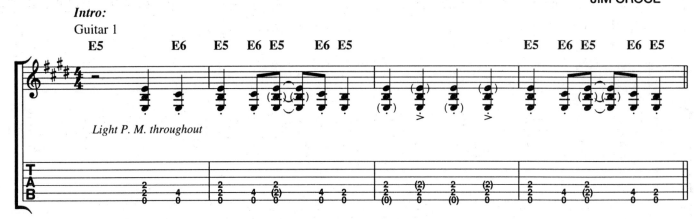

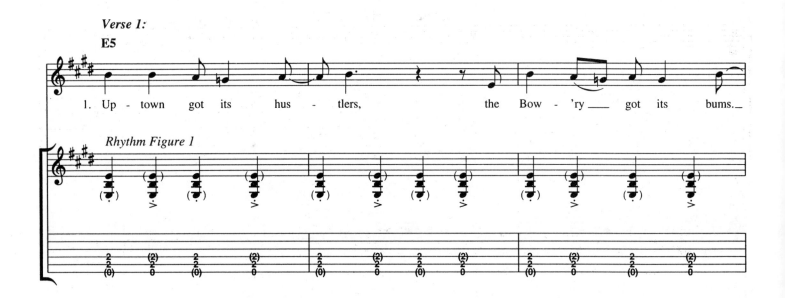

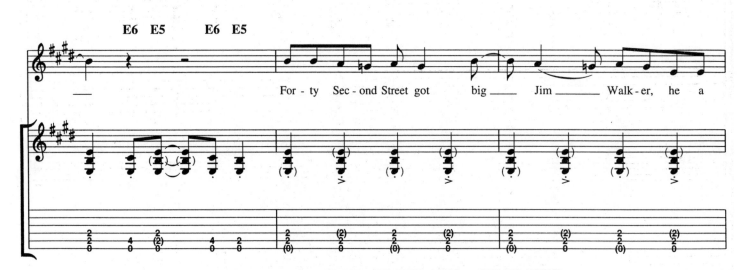

Chorus:

tug on Su - per - man's cape.   You don't   spit   in - to the

wind. _____   You don't   pull   the mask   off   the   old Lone Rang - er and you

Light P. M. - - - - - - - - - - - - - ⌡

Verses 2 & 3: With Rhythm Fig. 1 w/ ad-lib variations

*Background on Verse 3 only.
**On Verse 3 only.

*Piano adapted and arranged for Guitar 3.

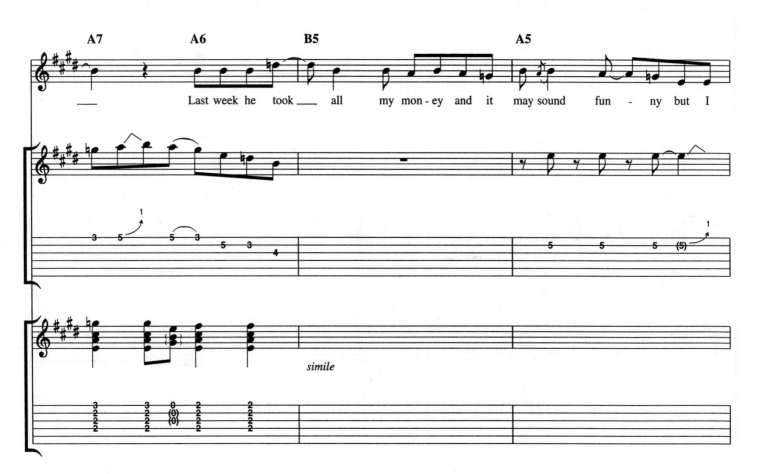

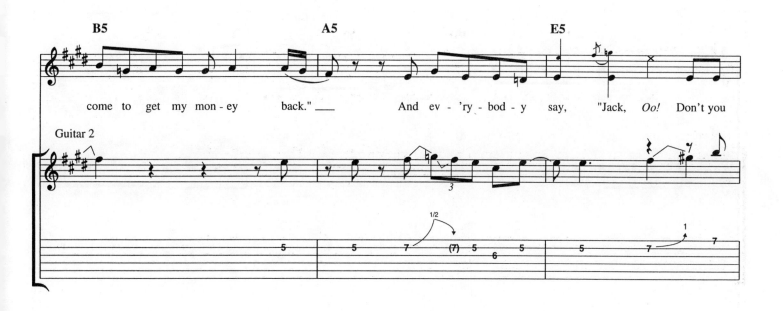

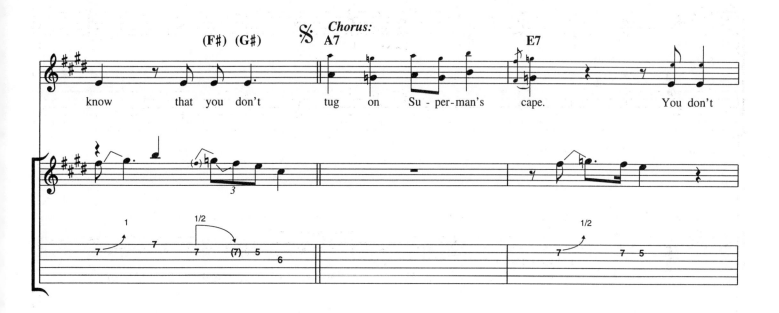

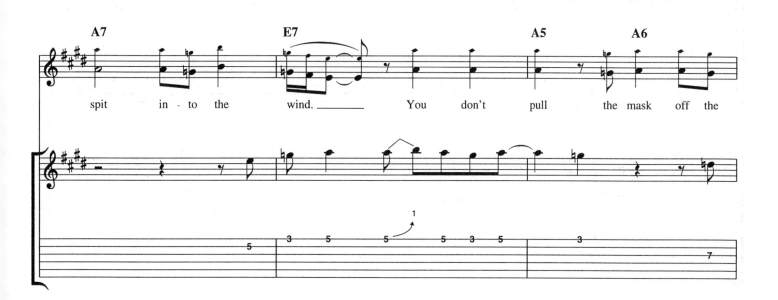

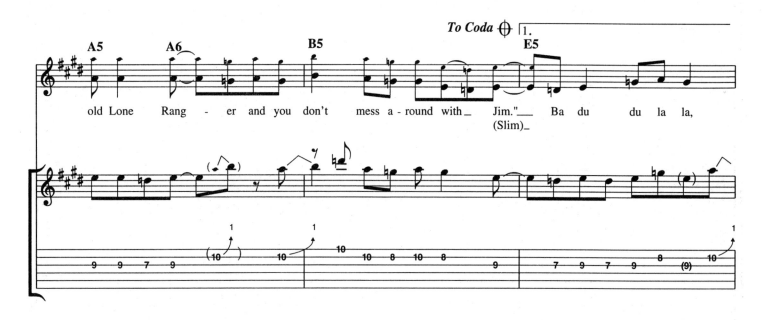

old Lone Rang – er and you don't mess a - round with _ Jim." _ Ba du du la la, (Slim) _

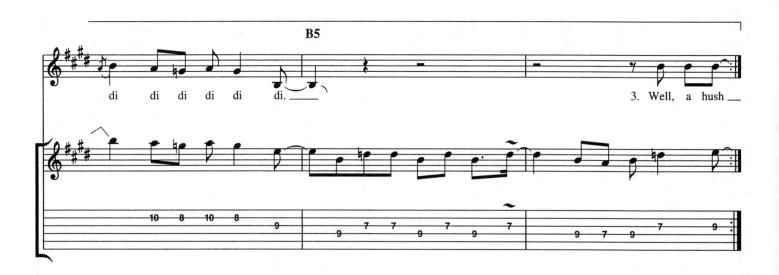

di di di di di di. _ 3. Well, a hush _

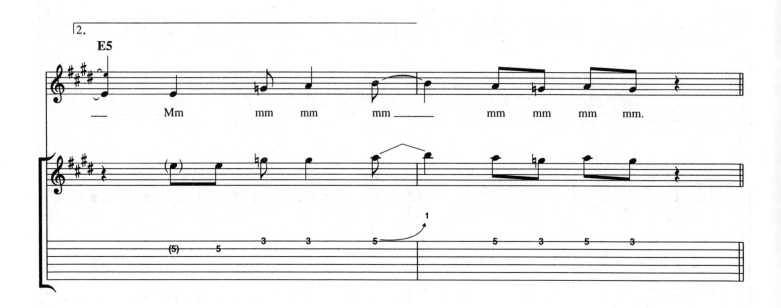

_ Mm mm mm mm _ mm mm mm mm.

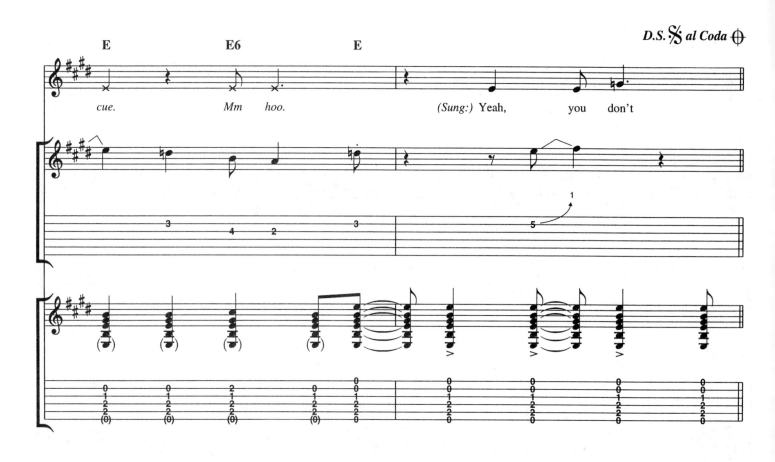

cue.   Mm   hoo.   *(Sung:)* Yeah,   you   don't

Coda ⊕

Outro: *With Rhythm Fig. 2 w/ ad-lib variations*

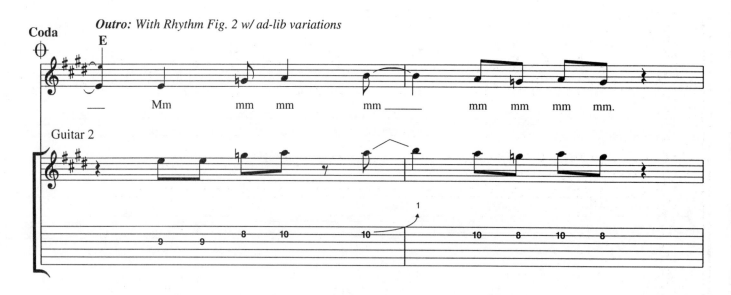

—   Mm   mm   mm   mm ____   mm   mm   mm   mm.

Guitar 2

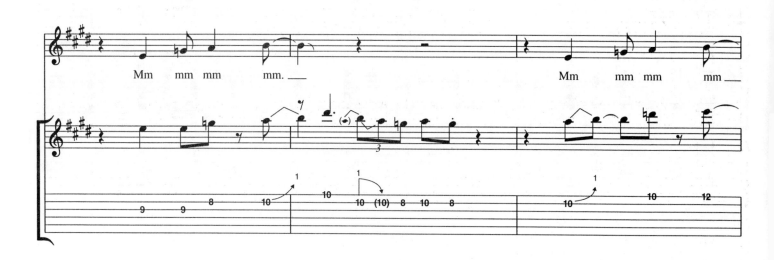

Mm   mm   mm   mm. ____   Mm   mm   mm   mm ____

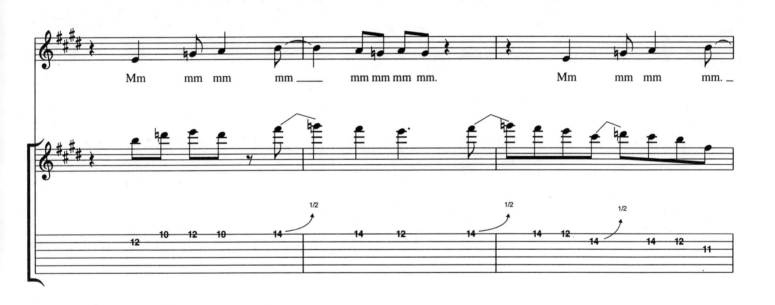

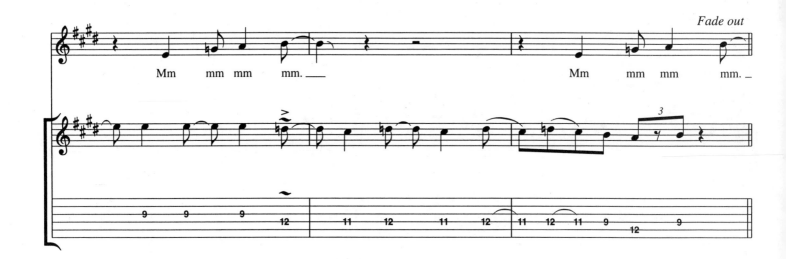

Fade out

Mm   mm   mm   mm. ___   Mm   mm   mm   mm. _

Additional lyrics

3. Well a hush fell over the poolroom,
    Jimmy come boppin' in off the street.
    And when the cuttin' were done,
    The only part that wasn't bloody was
    The soles of the big man's feet.
    Yeah, he were cut in 'bout a hundred places,
    And he were shot in a couple more.
    And you better believe they sung a diff'rent kind of story
    When a big Jim hit the floor.
    Oh. Now they say you don't...

    (To Chorus:)